A true worship experience does not just take place in the sanctuary on Sunday morning; it is a way of life. Leila Johnson understands this and shares her path to worship and to God so that others may examine their own steps to surrender and salvation.

Gwendolyn Mitchell, author of *House of Women*
Senior Editor of Third World Press

In *A Worship Experience* Leila Johnson takes us on a private journey into her heart, and allows us to see the pain and brokenness of her past. She shows us how God orchestrated her whole life in such a way as to bring healing and wholeness to her through worship.

In this powerful presentation we are given insightful instructions to help us on our journey; and we are challenged to make worship a lifestyle, rather than an event.

I highly recommend A Worship Experience to Pastors, Music Directors, Worship Leaders, Musicians, and Singers to enhance the worship experience of their various ministries and to transform congregations around the world into communities of true worshippers.

Pastor Alfonzo King Surrett Jr.
Author of *What Did You Really Say? Understanding the Destructive Effects of Profanity*

A Worship Experience
A guide for worshippers

Leila Johnson

His House Publishing
www.hishousepublishing.com

A Worship Experience
A Guide For Worshippers
Is Published By:

His House Publishing
www.hishousepublishing.com

Copyright notice:
A Worship Experience, A Guide For Worshippers © 2010 by Leila Johnson. All rights reserved. No part of this book may be reproduced in any form by any electronic or mechanical means (including photocopying, recording, or information storage and retrieval) now known or to be invented, without permission in writing from the author. For permission, please contact the author via email: leila@leilajohnsonministries.com

Printed in the United States of America on acid-free paper.
13 12 11 10 4 3 2 1

Cover Design: Minnie Watkins
Text and Layout: Solomohn N. Ennis, BFP.
Interior Image: Hands Prayer © 2010 TLorna

To contact author for bookings:
Leila Johnson
Email: leila@leilajohnsonministries.com
Website: leilajohnsonministries.com

For Information about Just Us Girls Women's Ministry:
Visit the website: www.jugswm.org

Dedication

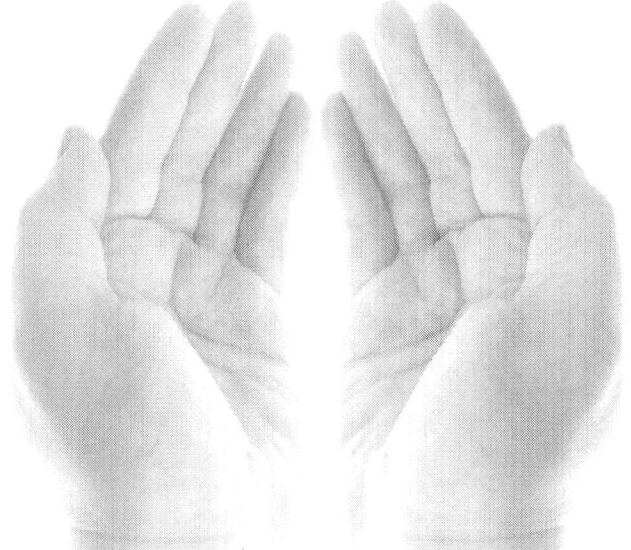

I dedicate this book to my two sons, Jason Michael Newman and Joshua Lavelle Newman. You have been a blessing to me and a gift from God. Jason, thank you for your support and love when things were hard for us as a family. Joshua, thank you for the words of truth you spoke to me challenging me to finish this book. Life has not always been easy for us, yet you hung in there with me with very little complaints. Thank you for your prayers and encouragement over the years. Your belief in me and my ministry has been a blessing to me. I have thoroughly enjoyed being your mother and have been delighted to have you as my sons. I love what God is doing in your lives.

I also dedicate this book in memory of my mom, Ruth A. Williams. Thank you for consistently reminding me that God has called and anointed me to the ministry of the word. Thank you for sharing your dreams and the revelations God gave you as it relates to me and my ministry. Thank you for telling me before you left to be with the Lord, that you loved me and that God was going to use me to do a great work for Him. Thank you for your support and your prayers for me and my sons over the years. You are greatly missed!

CONTENTS

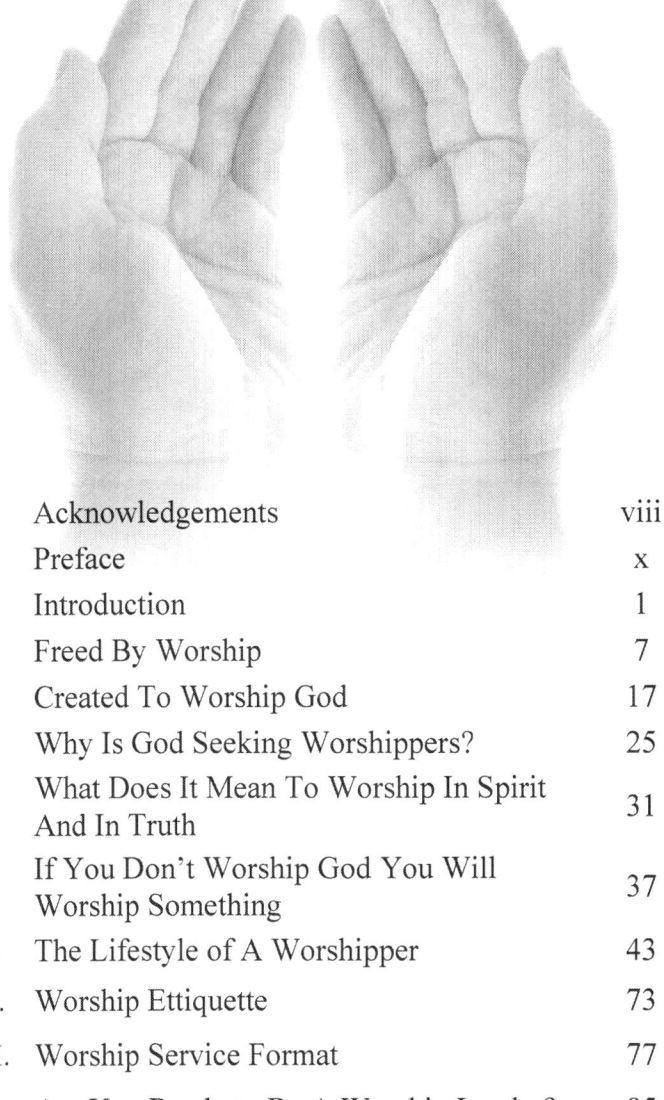

	Acknowledgements	viii
	Preface	x
	Introduction	1
I.	Freed By Worship	7
II.	Created To Worship God	17
III.	Why Is God Seeking Worshippers?	25
IV.	What Does It Mean To Worship In Spirit And In Truth	31
V.	If You Don't Worship God You Will Worship Something	37
VI.	The Lifestyle of A Worshipper	43
VII.	Worship Ettiquette	73
VIII.	Worship Service Format	77
IX.	Are You Ready to Be A Worship Leader?	85

ACKNOWLEDGEMENTS

To the Author and Finisher of my soul, Jesus Christ, thank you for never giving up on me.

To my closet and dearest friend, Deborah Ross, You believed in me from the day God knitted our hearts. You continued to speak words of life to me through all my death experiences. Thank you for your commitment and faithfulness to our friendship and to my ministry.

To my oldest friend Audrey Tolliver, words cannot express my gratitude for your time, your expertise, and using your sources to help me turn my dream into a well written manuscript. I'm grateful that we are still "girls together."

To my niece, Melodie Williams thank you for your patience and help, and to Cecelia Lovett for all the times that were unscheduled.

To my sister Shela Brown, Thank you for believing in my dreams, listening to me and praying that this book would come to fruition.

To my Brother Grady, thank you for encouraging, believing and reminding me of the ministry that God has placed in me.

To the rest of my Friends and Family who have supported this dream, I thank you more than words can say.

Preface

In *A Worship Experience* you will explore the journey of worship. It will challenge believers who desire to increase their worship life and give instruction and direction to those whom God has called to lead worship. Worship is not only about the music, the instruments or the songs, although these aspects help enhance your worship experience, worship is more about how well you live before the Lord. So many people in the body of Christ have taken for granted the importance of having a worship lifestyle. At the end of your day, ask yourself, "Do I leave God smiling or disappointed by my life?"

INTRODUCTION

Crack Skin

I ran as fast as my legs could carry me, "if he leaves me I am going to get a "crack skin" when he gets home." It was Wednesday evening, the night we had bible study at church. If you were not home when that Chevrolet station wagon pulled away from the curb you were in big trouble! "If only I had not taken that last turn of jump rope, I thought, I would have made it home in time." My father was one of the most kind hearted people I knew, but he was serious about two things, God and church; in that order. This meant for him and his eight children, reading scripture everyday and going to church whenever the church doors were open. It did not matter if it was a holiday, graduation, or birthday, you were going to church, that was not an option.

On church days if you were not home, Daddy never sent anyone to find you and he definitely was not going to look for you. He figured you knew the day of the week and the time, so if you were not in the car when he drove away expect a "crack skin" when he returned. As I stood on the sidewalk watching the Chevrolet station wagon turn the corner, my heart felt like it dropped to my trembling knees as my mind raced forward a couple of hours, to take a glimpse of what was to come.

"Crack Skin" was the metaphor used by my father to describe the discipline that would take place following acts of misbehavior and disobedience. It ranged from a whipping with a strap, to standing in the corner sometimes holding one leg, to writing scriptures 500 to 1000 times. You never really knew what you were going to get. I think my father relished the element of surprise. Nevertheless, whenever he said "I'm going to give you a crack skin," which was not often, (although my siblings would debate otherwise), it usually sent chills that birthed an expression of sheer panic and fear, accompanied by sweat and anxiety. I could almost feel the whips before I received them. I believe the anticipation of discipline was sometimes worse than the discipline itself. In one of my efforts to avoid a whipping, I fell into my father's lap, threw my arms around his neck and kissed him frantically all over his face telling him "I love you, I love you, I love you." My Daddy was not buying it. He chuckled, looked at me and said "I love you too but I'm still going to whip you."

As I look back on my father's disciplining techniques, I may not have agreed with all of his methods, but I do understand one clear thing, my "crack skins" were used to break or bend me so that I would go in a certain way. "Crack skins" often left me sad and upset yet humbled in total awareness of not only the situation, but how necessary the "crack skins" were, and that they worked for my good.

On occasion, after my whippings, I would write my father a letter of apology letting him know how sorry I was and how much I loved him, and in return he would let me know either in word or in deed that I was loved and forgiven. As I got older and examined the word crack it revealed something very interesting, crack means "broken" and the skin was "me" and isn't that what God does to us through the trials He allows and the corrections that we receive from Him? God breaks us and bends us to His way, and He does it with the kind heart of a father who is serious about our relationship with Him.

We take our lives and we envelop them in ways that leave God and his plans out. Then we get frustrated and irritated when our lives do not look a certain way or the results we were looking for are not evident. God in His never ending mercy looks past what we have done and configures the outcome to be what He had intended. During the whole process God allows us to receive "crack skin" experiences, giving us the opportunity to turn our lives around and get us back on course. Looking back at all the "crack skins" I received in my lifetime, including the few I received as a child, I now see that they have all been deliberate actions from a caring father, who like our Heavenly Father, knew that the plans he had for me were for good not evil to give me a future and a hope. In my life they have changed me tremendously for the better. Whether our circumstances are difficult or not so difficult, God still uses them all to draw us closer to Him to reveal, heal, deliver, restore and renew us.

Chapter I

Freed By Worship

My father was a bishop in our church organization and the pastor of our local church. In my younger years the denomination was very religious. Emphasis were more on the outer man and behavior than the inward man that speaks to our character. We were very traditional to say the least, very laid back and subdued. Many of the churches today sing a variety of worship songs with words displayed on remote control screens. Back when I was young, our church sang strictly hymns sung out of hymn books. Whenever we sang hymns related to going to heaven or being a good soldier for Christ, that is when you saw excitement and emotion. The congregation would sing these songs with so much joy and happiness, rocking back and forth, then they would began to jump and shout. Some would run and chairs would get knocked over in the process. There were times when the preacher did not get a chance to deliver the message because of the vast display of emotion. When the songs ended, people would be laid out on the floor with blankets over them. Some were in their seats swaying side to side crying, while others pivoted back and forth as if they were in a drunken stupor. The chairs that did not get knocked over due to the shouting were all out of place. Our church looked like a tornado hit it! I later realized that all that emotion did not seem to matter nor help when trouble came to my door.

Those early years in the church made me the most unprepared person for the life of turmoil and disappointment that I was later privy to. Do not misunderstand me, my father was a man of the word. He lived the life he preached. He taught his family scripture which gave me a good solid foundation. I remember my father saying from time to time "Leila, be good even if it kills you." I understand what he meant now, but then my interpretation was, "For appearance sake, put on a mask so no one sees the real you, and do what is right." With those words in the back of my mind, coupled with a denomination that focused on religion rather than a relationship with God, I thought God was strict, uncaring and unfeeling. I use to imagine God sitting in heaven sending people to hell because they wore jewelry, lipstick, colored nail polish, no sleeves and dresses above the knee. I was no more equipped to handle a failing marriage mixed with drugs and infidelity than I was all the heart break and depression that followed.

When you take Christianity and encase it with religion and tradition it will only produce self-righteousness and pride, rendering a person handicapped to their needs and feelings, and totally oblivious to the needs and feelings of others. It usually take drastic acts of sin to bring about what God has purposed and intended, whether you are the partaker of the sin or the one the sin was imposed upon. It was not until my marriage was falling apart, blame from ignorant bystanders, shame, embarrassment, fear and loneliness all wrapped around two innocent children that I came to realize that God was calling me to Himself, to a life of authentic worship.

I was a stay at home mom and my ex-husband worked as an Electrical Engineer. We had our problems but financially, our lives were comfortable. Marriage is already difficult with two people that love each other, but when one of the persons add adultery along with drugs and abuse to the equation, it is like trying to live on a sinking ship. Things began to spiral downward fast. We lost everything, all of our possessions, cars and furniture. We were living in California at the time, and had to move out of our home. With no place to go we moved to Chicago into my mother's house. While living there the lifestyle, lies, manipulation, adultery, including the drug abuse escalated. My ex-husband began to steal from me and family members. Drug dealers and addicts started knocking on our door all hours of the day and night looking for him. He stopped bringing home his pay check so I had to go to work. While I was at work, my ex-husband began taking my four-year-old son with him to crack houses to get high. In the meantime I was getting unkept promises and a lot of meaningless "I'm sorry's." I was not sleeping, barely eating, I was sad, depressed and full of anger. I wondered when was it going to stop and when was God going to intervene. I tried to shield my children from as much of the details as I could, but the lifestyle affected to much of their stability. One thing about living with someone who abuses drugs, your life is never private, everyone knows and sees what is going on and when they don't understand, they either criticize or blame. Someone asked me, "Leila, what did you do to make him turn to drugs?" A minister in my church said to me "Just suck it up Leila, it is not that bad you just have an unsaved husband," then the person began quoting the first part of 2 Cor. 7:14 "For the unbelieving husband is sanctified by the wife." I was so disappointed with the counsel. I thought no one understood what my life was like and no one was able to give me any guidance. The guilt and loneliness started to make me feel suicidal and one day I reached my limit! I couldn't take it anymore. I desperately needed to get out of that environment temporarily to give my children and myself a break. I packed up my kids along with a few things and drove from Chicago to Tennessee to stay with my sister and her husband for a while. In the midst of all the disappointment and pain I was experiencing, deep down within I knew God was calling me away. I did not realize it at the time but I was smack dab in the middle of one of the biggest "crack skins" of my life. God was using this experience to "break" me out of my religious, legalistic ways and "bend" me to a place of freedom and wholeness.

Tennessee held something very significant for me that changed my life forever. My first or second week there my sister invited me to go with her to a women's conference. I went that Friday night not knowing what I was about to encounter. The pastor's wife (I did not know it at the time) was leading worship and that was the first time that I had ever experienced that kind of emotion. It was far from what I was used to. It was not songs sung from lips that sang words out of duty. It was songs sung from hearts that serenaded a God that they knew and was devoted to. They raised their hands as if to reach for Him, they danced in the aisles as if no one was watching. As I looked around I was expecting chairs to get knocked over but that was not the case. This congregation praised and worshipped a God that they obviously adored. I looked up at my sister (I was still seated she was standing) and even she was clapping and waving her hands to the Lord. "When did she learn to do that I thought." I sat there in total amazement! How were they able to worship with such total abandonment?

As I sat there appearing unaffected by the worship and nonchalant by the presence of God, the Lord began speaking to me. "Leila, the one that is leading worship, is your twin." I asked God "What do you mean she is my twin, this lady looks nothing like me." To give you a description of this lady: she was about a foot shorter than me with hair reaching as far as the middle of her thigh, she was a size 2 or 4 and she was white. The only thing I saw that we had in common at the time was our music ability, we both could sing. As I sat there laughing to myself about God's sense of humor suddenly, this lady raised her voice in song holding a note as if to pour out her soul in worship to the Lord. It startled me a little. Then she quieted herself carefully, took off her shoes as if she was standing on sacred ground. She kneeled and bowed her face to the ground as if she was in the presence of the Almighty God. I felt the presence of God and fear ripped through my body like a bolt of lightning! The presence was so strong I had to hold on to the side of my seat. I was determined I was not going to get all emotional like her I was going to contain myself and not move a muscle.

Soon after she took her seat and the worship part of the service came to an end, to be honest, I was relieved. As the service proceeded, she was called back to the platform. It was then I realized that she was also the main speaker for the evening. Again the spirit of the Lord whispered "Leila, that is you." I cried inwardly to God and said "No

Lord, please don't ask me to do that. I'm a mess, my life is a mess, and besides, who would listen to me anyway?" God whispered to my spirit and said, "Leila, her story is your story." I asked God "What do you mean?" He told me to listen and pay attention. As she began to speak and share her testimony, I sat there frozen and stunned with tears running down my face. Her story was my story! She had experienced the same pain of drugs and adultery in her marriage as I. She had gone through the same heartache and depression. She had overcame suicidal thoughts and anger. I was floored! I asked God "How did she get to be so free in her worship?" God began to speak to me of His sovereignty. "I saw you in your pain, but I kept the pain from destroying you. I stood back and allowed the devastation in your life because it was needful for the plans I had for you. I have called you to the ministry of the word and to worship me in spite of your situation." Then the Lord said "Leila, your pain will be your pulpit." That is when the chains of defeat and religion fell off me. "I led you to Tennessee to show you why I created you and what I am going to do in you and through you." I sat there humbled in his presence.

After the message they had a time of prayer. I began to share my fears and discomforts to the Lord. I had not really done that before. Even though God knew my plight, I masked so much of it for appearance sake, I didn't know how to give it to him. That Friday night, I found myself in uncharted territory pouring out my heart to a God who loved and accepted me in a way I never knew or felt before. I began to lift my hands to the Lord. At first they were only shoulder length because I was aware of my surroundings, but as I continued to express to God, I began to feel that I had an audience of one, just Him and I. My hands found themselves lifted high over my head and I dropped to my knees in total surrender to Him. Although I never worshiped like that before it did not feel strange or awkward, it felt real and natural. God brought me back home that night, back to the reason He created me, back to the very purpose of my existence, which is worship. That night was like a metamorphosis. I went in one person, but I left totally different. I found who I was. I also found a new revelation of who God is in worship and it changed my life forever. I was set free!

CHAPTER II

Created To Worship God

Everyone who is called by My name, whom I have created for my glory; I have formed him, yes, I have made him. (Isaiah 43:7 NKJV)

This shall be written for the generation to come, that a people yet to be created may praise the Lord. (Psalm 102:18 NKJV)

Thou art worthy, O Lord, to receive glory and honour

and power: for thou hast created all things, and for thy pleasure they are and were created. (Revelation 4:11 KJV)

For of Him and through Him and to Him are all things, to whom be glory forever. Amen (Romans 11:36 NKJV)

All of humanity was created with a natural inborn ability to worship. That is God's plan, that is God's purpose, and that is God's intent. Although we were created with an inborn ability to worship, we are only supposed to give that worship to God. Worship is for His pleasure and His alone. *Isaiah 43:7* says I have created him for my glory. *Revelation 4:11* states, not only were we created by God, but we were created for his pleasure. God wants someone for Himself that will perform for Him at will. *Psalms 102:18* tells us that even the generations after us, our children, our grand children, our great grand children and so on, were created to worship God. God's desire is that the people He carefully crafted, would give Him praise, honor and glory. God wanted and still wants the full attention of all mankind. Deuteronomy says He's a jealous God, and only wants us to worship Him. It does not matter where we worship, it can be in our homes, on our jobs, in church, or at the store, God just wants us to worship Him.

So what is worship? Worship is love in its intimate state. Worship is a power source with extraordinary influence, that changes atmospheres and transforms human lives. While worship is very effective in its ways, it is also multi-functional in its capacity, for instance worship means to convey in words to sing and pray *(Psalm 66:2-3)*. It also means to press or force out like a shout *(Psalm 100:1)*. Worship means to represent by symbols and actions, for example with the display of banners *(Psalm 20:5)*, clapping your hands and lifting them in praise, *(Psalm 47:1 and Psalm 63:4)*, praising God in the dance and bowing to him *(Psalm 149:3 and Psalm 95:6.)*. Throughout the 150th chapter of Psalm, David says to praise God with different sorts of instruments; like the trumpet, lute, harp, timbrel, string instrument, flutes, loud cymbals, and clashing cymbals.

My father loved to hear the playing of instruments in our church service. He use to say, "Anything dead needs to be buried." Each one of his children (eight total) either played an instrument, sang vocally or both. The instruments in our church service that was not played by his children were made by his hands. Dad was so creative, he was a carpenter by trade. He would take a piece of wood, shape it into a paddle, get some pop bottle tops and hammer them flat (they were metal back then), and he would put holes in the center of them. Then he would take large nails and with his hammer nail the pop bottle tops to the piece of wood. He did not hammer the nails all the way through, he would leave space so the bottle tops would have room to move so when you shook them they would give the sound of a tambourine. We loved those "home made shingles"(that was the name mom called them). We would shake those shingles so hard during worship service sometimes the nails would loosen and the bottle tops would fly off them. I believe God enjoyed the sound from those shingles just as much as He enjoyed the harp that David played as long as they both were played with joy to Him, He was pleased.

Psalm 33:3 reminds us to enhance our gifts and talents and play skillfully with a shout of joy. Worship should be deliberate, intentional, and a conscious act. When Abraham was offering up Isaac, *Genesis 22:5* says Abraham said to his young men "Stay here with the donkey; the lad and I will go yonder to worship and we will come back to you." Worship should be non-stop like breathing; I will bless the Lord at all times and his praise shall continually be in my mouth. *(Psalm 34:1 NKJV)* Rejoice/celebrate in the Lord always. Again I will say rejoice *(Philippians 4:4 NKJV)*. Worship is not limited to age, race or any one group of people. We all were created and designed to worship God, so He needs to be the source of our worship. *John 3:16* says for God so loved the world that He gave his only begotten son, I previously mentioned that worship is love in its intimate state, I believe worship is our response to Gods "so" love. There is no way we can love God to the extent that He loves us, so He gave us an opportunity to respond to Him in an intimate way and that is through worship, loving God to the point that we give Him our all.

Since worship is reserved just for God, let's be careful we are not worshipping other people and things, and giving them our all, for example, our children, our jobs, food, sports, material possessions, drugs, alcohol, sex, and money. A person can become self absorbed, and worship attention, and appearances, or people focused, and worship acceptance and approval. There are even things that we are passionate about in our lives that we worship, like our gifts, talents and abilities. We worship titles, status, position, our ministries, and callings. We worship our problems and adversities. We will nurse them, rehearse them, obsess over them, until it is the first thing we think about in the morning and the last thing we think about at night. Our issues will pull the very life out of us if we allow them to. We were created to give God our all.

Worship is such a natural expression that when we find ourselves in its grasp there is a sense of belonging that engulfs the center of our being. Worshipping God is so intimate until it causes us to lose ourselves in its atmosphere and we begin to learn things about who we are and the object in which we worship. God created us for one purpose. That purpose and the very meaning for our existence is to worship God. It is the foundation on which humanity stands. Everything else we do is secondary. You may feel called to the ministry as a pastor or evangelist, but your number one purpose is to worship. You maybe called to sing, teach, work with children, feed the hungry, be a doctor, lawyer, scientist, etc. but your first direction is to worship and until you worship, you are not living at your best, fulfilled and whole. Worship is a place of completeness. When we worship God, we find who we are and we find our other giftings. Worship provokes a communicative exchange between the Creator and the creature. We talk to God, He talks to us, we tell Him our feelings He comforts us and reveals His plan for us. It's sad that people have died not realizing that their number one purpose was to worship God.

Chapter III

Why Is God Seeking Worshippers

But the hour cometh and now is, when the true worshippers shall worship the father in spirit and in truth: for the father seeketh such to worship him. (John 4:23 KJV)

To be created in the image of God, is an awesome attribute. How did we get from being created to worship God, to God is seeking someone to worship? It almost sounds like the scriptures are contradicting themselves. I have created you to worship, now I am seeking worshippers? Well what happened? When God created man, although our assignment was to worship He gave us a will, and with that will the ability to choose.

The will of man can be on one hand, very welcoming, pleasant, and refreshing while on the other hand very deliberate, intentional, stubborn, strong and even intimidating. Our wills are at the root of who we really are.

If we stop and take a look at ourselves, who we are, where we are, and what we have done, it is the direct result of our will. We were given power and strong determination to function as human beings. However, some of us are not exactly making our creator proud with our results. The will of man can be so complex, but it is so needed to carry out the purpose and direction of God. That is what God had in mind when he gave us a will.

God created us with a choice, and man has exercised that choice. As a result many have diverted from the original plan of God, gone their own way, done their own thing, looking for a sense of belonging. Inwardly knowing something is missing, man comes back to God but satan does not want him to give God his all. Satan hates worship. He whispers to man's desperately seeking intellect that worship has to look a certain way and act a certain way. Isaiah says it clearly: *Wherefore the Lord said, forasmuch as this people draw near me with their mouth, and with their lips do honour me, but have removed their heart far from me, and their fear toward me is taught by the precept of men. (Isaiah 29:13 NKJV)*. Isaiah basically prophesied that Jesus would be searching for worshippers because man have come near to God with their mouth and honored Him with their lips but their hearts are far from Him. Their worship is made up only of rules taught by men.

The fall of man was predicted and it was an inevitable event. Even though we were created to worship, somehow our worship is done out of duty and not from the heart. We draw near to God or we make steps toward God but it is not about Him at all and God knows it. In our hearts "Lucifer" still lives and causes us to be motivated by works, accomplishments, talents and gifts. We tend not to think worship is a daily life style, therefore it only comes to mind as it relates to our Sunday morning services when the music starts and the words appear on our fancy remote control screens in our updated remodeled sanctuaries.

The women said, "Sir I perceive that You are a prophet. Our fathers worshipped on this mountain, and you Jews say that in Jerusalem is the place where one ought to worship." Jesus said to her, "Woman believe Me, the hour is coming when you will neither on this mountain nor in Jerusalem, worship the Father. You worship what you do not know, we know what we worship for salvation is of the Jews."(John 4:19-22 NKJV) Worship can become all about a particular place, for a specific time, and done in a specific way. If you isolate and designate worship, you have missed worship altogether. The location of worship is not nearly as important as the attitude of the worshippers. Jesus said to the woman *"You worship what you do not know,"* but He is also saying those words to us today. Do we worship who we do not know? Have we allowed God to walk so close to us until we know Him as a healer, a peacemaker, or a restorer? Have we allowed God to sit as King of our lives and make decisions through us? Do we really rely on Him? Can we trust Him to know what's best for us even if we don't receive our desired outcome? The woman said, *"I perceive that you are a prophet."* She did not know for certain because she never allowed Him to speak into her life and we are no different. We claim God is the Lord of our lives and we run to Him with our never ending issues, yet we still hold all the answers and will not release ourselves to His solutions.

Worship is about becoming one with Christ. How can we ever come to know Him if we are only on the sidelines perceiving who He is? That is why God is seeking worshippers. One cannot just intellectually know God. We must seek Him like He is seeking us. The way to do that is reset your priorities and make God the center and core of your life. *Out of the abundance of the heart the mouth speaks (Mathew 12:34).* Ask yourself, "Is God speaking from the core of my heart when I open my mouth?" *Out of your heart speaks the issues of life (Proverbs 4:23).* Take a honest look at your life, where you are today, what you have accomplished or not, all your decisions: family, work, school, ministry and personal, and what you desire to do. Has God been the center of every issue? The concern should not be the act of worship but the object of our worship. It is God's heart that He become the object of your worship. *I am the Lord, that is my name; and my glory I will not give to another, Nor my praise to carved images. (Isaiah 42:8 NKJV).*

Chapter IV

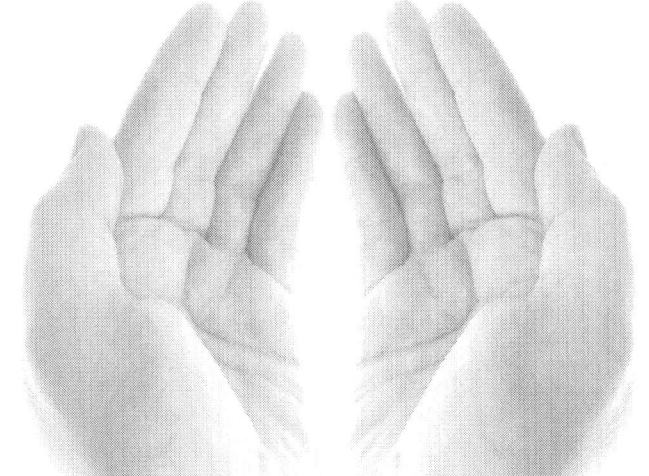

What Does It Mean To Worship In Spirit And In Truth

God is a spirit and they that worship him must worship him in spirit and in truth.(John 4:24 NKJV)

Thus says God the Lord, Who created the heavens and stretched them out, who spread forth the earth and that which comes from it, who gives breath to the people on it and spirit to those who walk on it. (Isaiah 42:5 NKJV)

God is a spirit and that means He is not a physical being limited to one place. He is everywhere. We live in a time that gives us the freedom and wonderful opportunity to worship God and enjoy His presence anywhere, anytime, anyplace with very little restrictions. *It is God the Lord who gives us the breath and the spirit to walk on this earth so let us not take advantage of this wonderful gift (Isaiah 42:5 NKJV),* use that gift with a spirit of sovereignty and authenticity. Our worship must be sincere and honest before the Lord and must not be mistaken for emotions. That is what Christ meant by worshipping Him in spirit and in truth. This is a time for self examination. Are you living a life of truth or are you living a lie? Do you lift up holy hands or are your hands filthy with secret sin? There are churches today that are filled with people and leaders whose worship is nothing but a display of ardent, high strung emotion instead of a demonstration of a passionate servant showering love and praise on the God they serve.

Satan is the "prince of the power of the air" *(Ephesians 2:2).* His domain is in the atmosphere *(Ephesians 6:12),* the earth and the seas *(Revelation 12:7-12)*. That is where he lives, breathes, and gain his momentum. Whatever you speak in the atmosphere if it is negative, satan can build and magnify it to work against you, which is why we need to speak life and blessings and choose our words carefully. God has given him authority to dwell in darkness including the darkness that appears in a believers heart. When we lead worship with a lifestyle that is questionable, we lead the people in a worship that is not coming from truth but from deception. When that happens we open the door for demonic forces to be released in our worship service and satan can control the atmosphere. Every song that you sing that contains the words "King" or "Lord" is then given to satan and he is exalted. You may think worship happened because the people are emotional but it is just a display of idolatrous worship. That is not the power of God. Healing, deliverance, and peace are not being experienced from the people, just excitement. They will leave the way they came unless the Leader of Worship, Pastor or Minister can break through that atmosphere so that the people can receive a change. It takes discernment and the direction of the Holy

Spirit to minister on the heels of such satanic influence. Although it can be done why go through all the trouble.

I beseech you therefore brethren by the mercies of God that you present your bodies a living sacrifice, holy, acceptable unto God which is your reasonable service. And be not conformed to this world but be ye transformed by the renewing of your minds that you may prove what is that good and acceptable and perfect will of God (Romans 12:1-2 NKJV). You cannot lead anyone where you have not been. My mentor said something that I am compelled and encouraged to live by, "Fruit gives you credibility," your lifestyle will deem you credible or expose your sins. How many credible worshippers do we really have in the body of Christ. If we were to go home with you, go to work with you, hang out with you, will we label you as credible? What is being said about you, that if known, would it cause encouragement to others or harm to others? Paul in *Romans 12 :1-2* makes a serious declaration; use your bodies to serve and obey God, stop mentally accommodating worldly ways and views, dedicate your mind to God's truth and it will produce a life that can stand the test of time, resist temptation and allow the Holy Spirit to guide and shape your thoughts and behavior. We have to be extremely careful as worshippers and as worship leaders. If our relationship with God is not where it should be, we can stand in the way of the Holy Spirit moving in our lives and congregations. *Behold you desire truth in the inward parts, and in the hidden part you will make me to know wisdom (Psalm 51:6 NKJV).*

It is not where you worship but how you worship. Is your worship genuine and true?

Chapter V

If You Don't Worship God You Will Worship Something

One thing the enemy cannot do is steal your worship or your praise because that is what God created you for. However, he will divert your attention to get you to worship and praise someone or something else. This redirection of worship by the enemy has also caused our weekly worship times to be sedated, watered down and filled with religious jargon, rituals, emotion and hype.

As a result, real worship has been abandoned and neglected.

Man has been built with the need and inborn natural ability to connect with God. The absence of that connection will cause man to find a substitute. You see we were created in the image and likeness of God. We were also given power and authority, to the point where we can have what we say, call those things that are not as though they were, and can ask anything in Jesus name and it shall be given. With that in mind we need to be careful who we give our allegiance to because the minute we release worship is the second we receive a god. The reason I say that is when you worship God it gives Him permission to be your God and then He Lords over you. When you worship people, money, drugs, approval and even your job it gives those things permission to lord over you. Gods are formed in our lives out of habitual behavior, but also out of loyalty, faithfulness and sincere devotion which is worship. When the evidence of those gods become obvious in our lives, we find ourselves caught in their traps, unable to escape their control, and lost in their manipulation and power over us.

Worship is more than an expression, worship is extremely powerful. Worship involves all five of our senses; our taste (your appetite, what your prefer), our smell, our touch (your discernment, what you do), our hearing (who we listen to) and our seeing (what you pay attention to). When we begin to worship, our souls and our spirits become liberated with a sense of self-abandonment that leaves us ripe and open as our hearts become fertile soil to the sower. This is awesome groundwork for the working of the Holy Spirit, but on the other hand if yielded to the enemy the land will demonstrate disaster for us. We can become dominated by so many things in so many areas, so we need to submit to the power of God that calls us into daily relationship with Him.

Then He said to them all, if anyone desires to come after Me, let him deny himself and take up his cross daily and follow Me (Luke 9:23 NKJV). In other words, whoever purposes in his heart to walk after God, let him disown self, distractions, and lay aside any hindrances. Let him do what it takes to daily pursue God and his ways in everything he does. That is real worship! If we do not deny our self and flesh, then self and flesh will take control and find another object of worship. We cannot lay worship down and pick it up when it suits us and expect the Lord's blessing in our lives. If we desire to follow after God He will lead us in good pastures, daily. *You will show me the path of life; In your presence is fullness of joy. At your right hand are pleasures forevermore (Psalm 16:11).* Once we decide to follow God and give Him our worship, He then reveals to us the path of life and the path of independence which requires total dependence on Him. God will reveal to us how to have freedom and a life filled with enjoyment in every area of our lives. I believe that is why God only wants us to worship Him and not anyone or anything else.

God wants us to release worship to Him because he wants to be our God. *Thou shalt have no other gods before me (Exodus 20:3).* For thou shalt worship no other god: for the Lord whose name is Jealous, is a jealous God *(Exodus 34:14).* God is very territorial. He does not want any other creature or creation to house the section in our hearts that is reserved just for Him. He wants us to be captivated and intoxicated only by Him.

Jesus, the potter, wants us on His wheel. What a great experience to be caught in the clutch of the almighty God, totally surrendered to Him as He molds and shapes us. He wants to sit in our center so He can direct and control the traffic that goes in and out of our lives. God is not interested in halfhearted commitment, partial obedience, and the leftovers of our time and money. He desires our full devotion, not little bits and pieces of our lives. Worship whether in word or deed is the most intimate expression of love, honor and reverence that we can give God, and He deserves it.

Chapter VI

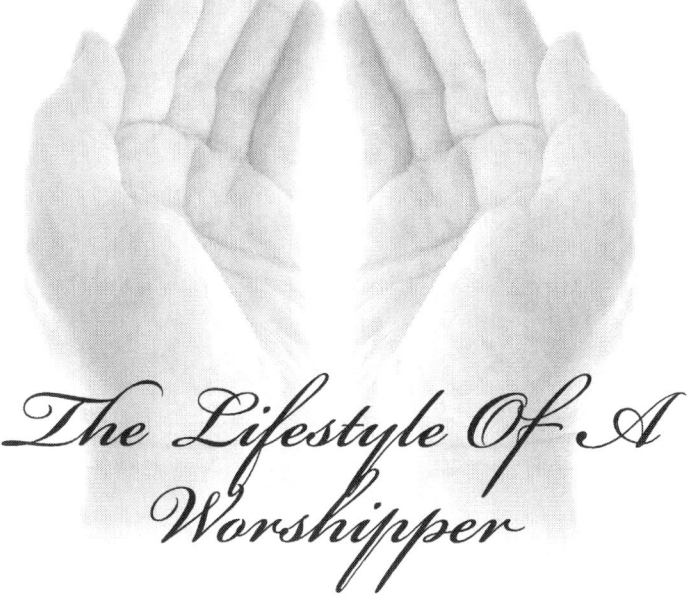

The Lifestyle Of A Worshipper

But the Lord, who brought you up from the land of Egypt with great power and an outstretched arm, Him you will fear, Him you shall worship and to Him you shall offer sacrifice. 2Kings 17:36 NKJV

The judgment of God is so clear and relevant in the Old Testament. It is a wonder why the people back then did not take Him as seriously as they should have. The degrees of God's judgment ranges from castration to stoning, to burning, and to cutting off heads. All these incidents were witnessed by the people of the Old Testament, yet, it seemed they lived in total oblivion of these consequences of disobedience and took God for granted. I am not sure if it was due to their lack of faith or if it was just God hardening their hearts so His glory could be performed and revealed. Nevertheless, God has not changed nor has His word. Times have changed, believers have changed to the point that they have watered down the gospel, the word of God, and have taken certain aspects about God for granted, but God has not changed.

I so appreciate the love of God that covers our wrongs and lovingly graces us back to Him. I adore His mercy that justifies us and removes all guilt and shame and makes us whole spiritually and emotionally. God has His limits. Take advantage of His kindness while you have a chance. He is still a God that chastises. Some of us have become misguided as it relates to the judgment of God, and the results have been disastrous for us. We are unprepared and then when judgment happens, we blame God, we say it's not fair, we become angry, and we put Him in the corner with our backs to Him as if He is the one at fault. *Do not be deceived, God is not mocked; for whatever a man sows, that he will also reap (Galatians 6:7 NKJV)*. Let's take a close look at our lives. Are we reaping a harvest that we have sowed? Sometimes when we ask God for direction and we do not get the answer we seek, we make our own choices and the results have left us hurt, disappointed, or like me devastated with two small children fending for myself and totally unprepared for the cold lonely hard life ahead.

My father did not put a lot of emphasis on higher education as far as his girls were concerned, but he never discouraged us either if it was what we desired. I went to college but I did not finish. If I had finished, although my decision was out of the will of God to marry at that time, I would have been better prepared financially when the marriage fell apart. The choices and decisions we make no matter what they are will shape our future and the consequences can prove to be brutal!

Ezekiel, who was a prophet, warns Israel of coming doom due to their continued disregard of God and His laws. *"Now the end has come upon you, and I will send my anger against you; I will judge you according to your ways, and I will repay you for all your abominations. My eye will not spare you, nor will I have pity; but I will repay your ways...then you shall know that I am the Lord"! (Ezekiel 7:3-4 NKJV).* If we take a look at our lives and the lives of some in the body of Christ because of disobedience, many are experiencing the undeniable judgment of God. Verses like these in Ezekiel, serve as a reminder for us to pause and terminate living unconsciously about the full character of God. We need to be very mindful that God in his loving, merciful way commands a behavior from us that is neither difficult, carnal, convoluted, nor lifeless but simple, holy, unquestionable and spirited. God not only commands it, but it is the desire of His heart. *Behold, you (God) desire truth in the inward parts (Psalms 51:6).* God is calling for those who desire the same. *If anyone desires to come after Me, let him deny himself and take up his cross and follow me (Matthew 16:24 NKJV).* I believe coming after God and following Him takes a specific mindset and lifestyle.

Worship can be extroverted in its context (the outward expression or what appears physically), but the purpose or the emphasis of worship was meant to be more introverted than extroverted. An extroverted worshipper asks "Did I sing right? Are they looking at me? If not, I must do something or say something to be noticed, I must lift my hands so they will know I am a worshipper, I must show them I dance well and play my instruments skillfully," their interest is on the outward. An introverted worshipper's interest is first on the inward expression of worship than the outward expression of worship. An introverted worshipper says "before I sing, lift my hands, dance, or display any musical talent/abilities, I must first make certain that I'm keeping my heart with all diligence because that is where the root of worship begins" *(Proverbs.4:23 MSG)*. Paul writes *I beseech (I earnestly ask you) therefore brethren, by the mercies of God that you present your bodies a living sacrifice, holy acceptable to God which is your reasonable service (Romans 12:1 NKJV)*.

The Message Bible version of Romans 12:1 says, So

here's what I want you to do, God helping you: Take your everyday, ordinary life—your sleeping, eating, going to work, and walking around life—and place it before God as an offering. To be a living sacrifice means to voluntarily offer yourself to God, to walk a certain way, to make a stand. One of the Greek meanings of a living sacrifice or offering is to become an "Altar," a place of sacrifice before God, a place where God can perform His will and demonstrate His love.

I believe one of the greatest stories of worship is found in *1Kings 18: 21,31-39*. This story points out some specific ways and instructions for living the life of a worshipper. Let's take at look at the scripture and see what it says to us.

And Elijah came to all the people, and said," How long will you falter between two opinions?" If the Lord is God, follow him, but if Baal, follow him. But the people answered him not a word.

And Elijah took twelve stones, according to the number of tribes of the sons of Jacob, to whom the word of the lord had come, saying "Israel shall be your name" Then with the stones he built an altar in the name of the Lord; and he made a trench around the alter large enough to hold two seahs of seed.

And he put the wood in order, cut the bull in pieces, and laid it on the wood, and said, "Fill four water pots with water, and pour it on the burnt sacrifice and on the wood. Then he said, "Do it a second time," and they did it a second time; and he said, "Do it a third time," and they did it a third time. So the water ran all around the altar; and he also filled the trench with water.

And it came to pass, at the time of the offering of the evening sacrifice, that Elijah the prophet came near and said "Lord God of Abraham, Isaac and Israel, let it be known this day that You are God in Israel and I am your servant and that I have done all these things at your word. Hear me, O Lord, hear me, that this people may know that You are the Lord God, and that You have turned their hearts back to you again."

Then the fire of the Lord fell and consumed the burnt sacrifice, and wood and the stones and the dust, and it licked up the water that was in the trench.

Now when all the people saw it, they fell on their faces; and they said, "The Lord, He is God! The Lord, He is God!" (1 Kings 18:21,31-39 NKJV)

This was a great display of the power of God. Elijah was not only part of a demonstration to prove the power of God, but he came to repair "the altar" that had been torn down, and restore it back to God. This was the altar David and the true people of God used years before to offer sacrifices to the Lord (read the book of 1 Kings). Because of disobedience and neglect, beginning with King Solomon, the people replaced it with altars built to Baal and other gods. The altar was left in major need of repair. Today, God wants to restore altars back to him, but one of the first things we must do is make a decision, make a stand!

Make A Decision

And Elijah came to all the people, and said," How long will you falter between two opinions?" If the Lord is God, follow him; but if Baal, follow him. But the people answered him not a word.

The people were silent! The reason they were indecisive is because their leader, Ahab, was indecisive. He could not decide whether to serve God or Baal. God was fed up with the indecisiveness of the people. So Elijah challenged the people, "Are you going to serve God or Baal?" You cannot serve two masters. God needs to see in word and action that people are serious about following him. *Joshua 24:15* says choose ye this day whom you will serve. *Rev 3:15:16* talks about being hot or cold and not luke warm or you will make God sick! (paraphrased) This scripture is not saying that God prefers you to be saved or unsaved, it speaks specifically to the character of an individual. You see, there were hot and cold waters that ran through the city of Laodecea. The hot waters were useful for healing purposes and the cold waters were for, refreshing purposes. The question is are you useful or are you refreshing because if you are neither, you are of no use to God and you make Him sick. First you must decide that it is God that you will worship, then you must demonstrate that decision by being someone useful; meaning not lazy but dependable, active and busy, a person that can be trusted, or demonstrate someone refreshing meaning someone that is pleasant and kind, easily to be entreated, pleasant to be around, someone that brings encouragement, someone that speaks the heart of God. When you have made the decision to worship God then begin to put your life in order.

Order

Then Elijah said to all the people Come near to me. So all the people came near to him and he prepared the altar of the Lord that was broken down. And Elijah took twelve stones, according to the number of the tribes of the sons of Jacob, to whom the word of the lord had come, saying "Israel shall be your name."

Elijah took twelve stones, one for each of the tribes of

Jacob, the same Jacob to whom God had said, From now on your name is Israel, He built the stones into the altar in honor of God. And he said, *Thy name shall be called no more Jacob, but Israel: for as a prince hast thou power with God and with men, and hast prevailed. Gen 32:28 (KJV)*

Elijah began building the altar with the twelve stones. Why twelve? Twelve means order. Sometimes in our Christian life we can lose our way, and get discouraged. What needs to happen quickly so we don't lose our way is stop and meditate on what God has done in our life and draw our focus back to Him so we can keep our perspective. Our life must have order or a point of focus so God can move. In First Kings they lost their way and Elijah was trying to take them back to not only when God changed Jacob's name to Israel, but a time when God called him a prince and when he had power with God and man and prevailed. Elijah was taking them back to a time when there were no kings and God was their King. A time when enemies were defeated and victories were won. A time before things got out of control, before the twelve tribes scattered, a time when God was not foreign to them and they were familiar with His works. Elijah was trying to bring them back to a place that they knew, back to God.

For some of us our altars/lives are in major need of repair and getting from one place to another is all we can handle. We have allowed other kings to rule and control our lives. We have been through so much and have strayed so far from the path God intended, until some things in our lives have become unrecognizable. If we can do like Elijah and remember, remember the good times, remember the day God came into our lives and saved us from a life of sin and ourselves. If we can remember the healing power of God and His ability to restore and deliver. Remember that we are not alone and that God has never abandoned us. The word of God says we are an over comer by the blood of the Lamb and by the word of our testimony. Testify to yourself, you don't need an audience. I guarantee you if you play back the videos of all that God has done in your life, you will find yourself caught up in the presence of

God worshipping and loving Him. Let's be honest with ourselves, things have not always been bad. God has come through and He will again. Bring things in order and remember God. Remembering puts God back in His rightful place in your life!

Build A Trench

Then with the stones he built an altar in the name of the Lord; and he made a trench around the altar large enough to hold two seahs of seed.

This is where it gets a little strange. What was Elijah doing? Trenches around altars were not the norm back then when it came to building an altar. So why did Elijah build a trench, what was he thinking, what was the purpose? Not only did he build a trench but he built it large enough to hold two seahs of seed. There appears to be several meanings to the dimensions of "two seahs of seed." In the Torah the dimensions of an area that requires two seahs of seed is equivalent in size to the courtyard of the "Mishkan." This was a portable tent of worship that was situated in the center of the Israelite encampment in the desert after the exodus from Egypt. Another Hebrew finding stated that two seahs equaled 100 cubit feet long & 100 cubit feet wide. The Standard Christian bible says two seahs of seed was equivalent to 4 gallons of water. I am not certain which measurement was used by Elijah, but I am certain that it was quite out of the ordinary. Nevertheless, Elijah was specific and strategic in building this structure that was uncommon both in culture and capacity.

A trench is a ditch or channel dug in the ground. Trenches today are used in the military to protect the troops from enemy fire and shelter them from artillery.

Our purpose for building a trench in our life is to hide and protect us from enemy fire. Any time God blesses or gives us peace, joy, healing, or encouragement, the enemy is on his way to steal it! Be an Elijah, do what it takes to protect yourself. Get specific and strategic. Build a place of hiding and protection. Build it deep enough to cover you and your loved ones. Get aggressive toward the enemy.

Stop letting the enemy steal territory in your life!!! Get fed up and tell him enough is enough!

Worship God regardless of your circumstance. Don't worry, worship. Don't get upset and angry, worship. Clapping hurts the enemy's ears. Praise in the midst of problems, confuses the devil. Lifting up your hands with palms open, surrenders the situation to the almighty King and cuffing your hands means you want to receive what God has for you in that moment. Stop complaining and use some thank you's and hallelujahs and put the enemy on the run! Stand up to him let him know you are not scared of him. *Greater is He that is in you than he that is in the world (1 John 4:4).* Plead the blood of Jesus to mark your territory. Set a boundary and dare the enemy to cross it. Meditate on God's grace and keeping power. Man or woman of God, no one can do it for you. Build your own trench and when you do, you will witness the manifestation of the power of God

Sacrifice

And he put the wood in order, cut the bull in pieces, and laid it on the wood,

This is where sacrifice comes in, you MUST be willing to sacrifice and even go through sacrifices from time to time. Without sacrifices you cannot and will not grow as a Christian. Sacrifice means I am willing to forfeit or relinquish everything for the sake of something or someone else. Sacrifice takes you out of the picture so another can be on display. Sacrifice makes room for something greater to take place. Sacrifice helps to shape us into what God intended for us to be.

Sacrifice is inevitable when it comes to worship. They go hand in hand. You cannot have one without the other. Sacrifice is anything that is consecrated and offered to God that costs us something. Once the decision is made to worship it is going to cost you. Something comes out of you in worship, an exchange is made.

I remember a specific time praying desperately for God to move in my life. I was filled with worry, feeling sorry for myself and sinking deep into a depressive state. I wanted and needed deliverance. One day as I was praying to God for help the Holy Spirit led me on a three day fast and I obeyed without hesitation. I went without food and water. I didn't watch any TV, I just read my bible, prayed, listened to gospel music and stayed in the presence of God. I did not go anywhere which was easy because at the time I was a stay at home mom. I prepared myself so that aside from the regular everyday duties the only major activity I did was take care of my oldest son who was two at the time. I have experienced this type of fast before, witnessed the hand of God move in my life, and my relationship with the Lord went deeper. I was in need of an outpouring of the Holy Spirit again. I was desperate, needing something, anything I could get from the Lord. I was open and ready. Three days was a long time to go without water and periodically I would get weak but every time I did, I would read the word of God and I would gain strength. I began to feel my body getting nourishment and feeling energized.

By the middle of the third day my body was weak and I was moving slowly physically but my spirit man was strong and I was determined to stick it out to the end. I told God, "I need a miracle, I need a change in my life and I am not going to eat or drink until the end of this fast." I felt like Jacob when he was wrestling with the angel "I'm not going to let you go until you bless me." God healed me and began the ground work for ministry. I was not expecting the ministry part I just wanted more of God but God always saves you for someone else. He always has something great in mind when He blesses us.

You also as living stones are being built up a spiritual house, a holy priesthood, to offer up spiritual sacrifices acceptable to God through Jesus Christ (1Peter 2:5). Living Stones...stones are not live creatures to begin with so what was Peter getting at? Stones were used in earlier times for building and construction. They were used more often than natural rock because stones were, easier to shape, develop and mold. Stones were basically easier to work with. In light of this scripture, Peter not only referred to

Christians as stones but stones that are alive, with a pulse, that move, and are energetic and interactive. Stones that get involve, and are obedient, stones that listen, and are willing to be accountable, teachable and approachable. Living stones allow the Holy Spirit to direct them. They do not take for granted the privilege and responsibility of offering up spiritual sacrifices (worship) that are acceptable to God. If you are a stone, sacrifice is not foreign to you. So ask yourself, "Are you natural rock or are you a stone?"

Water

And said, "Fill four water pots with water, and pour it on the burnt sacrifice and on the wood. Then he said, "Do it a second time," and they did it a second time; and he said, "Do it a third time," and they did it a third time. So the water ran all around the altar; and he also filled the trench with water.

Water = "THE WORD OF GOD"

The word of God in the life of a believer is just as crucial as the blood to the human body, without it you die! Elijah knew if he did not drench that altar with the water (word of God) he would not have a chance. Skeptics may have thought it strange that Elijah used water on something he was going to burn later. But Elijah was very familiar with how God operates. God performs everywhere He sees His word. It was an honor to God to see His word poured out on the altar. It honors God and makes Him act out when He can see His word in us. Many perform in our churches today without having the word live through them but it is only a performance because God sees the heart. Drench your life with the word of God, read it, meditate on it, memorize it, live it and quote it over and over again. God moves by His word and where ever He sees His word. Make God's word a priority in your life! Be sensitive to the word of God and to what it speaks to you, your family and your surroundings, and pray the word of God in those areas. Scripture memorization is vital. Quoting scripture is a powerful tool that dismantles the works and plans of the enemy and gives power, strength and hope to the believer. Speaking scripture reaffirms your covenant with God and His covenant with you. This is one of the reasons why the devil hates to hear scripture and hates to see us read and live out scripture in our life.

Without the word living within you, you cannot hear the voice of God. The word of God is a guide for the life of a Christian. It instructs, warns, encourages and uplifts the believer. Hold the word precious to your heart like David says in *Psalms 119:133* (paraphrased) Lord, direct my steps by your word, and don't allow any iniquity to have dominion over me. David valued the word of God. Stay drenched with God's word. You cannot pour out if YOU have not been wet.

Humility

And it came to pass, at the time of the offering of the evening sacrifice, that Elijah the prophet came near and said "Lord God of Abraham, Isaac and Israel, let it be known this day that You are God in Israel and I am your servant and that I have done all these things at your word.

Elijah knew he reached a pivotal moment that would have an impact on the rest of his life and the life of the people. He understood that the rest of what was about to take place had everything to do with his posture, his ability to humble himself. After you have fed yourself on the word of God allow the word to make changes and adjustments without any interference. *1Peter 5:5* says to be clothed with humility. That means I must make a choice and choose humility, take it and put it on and wear it everywhere I go. Humility speaks to three areas: authority, position and response. Take a look again at verse 36:

"You are God"—Elijah declared God's authority.

Humility is not about you. Who are the authorities in your life? Do you acknowledge them? Humility not only recognizes but gives respect, honor, and appreciation to the authority figures in our lives. Humility is a choice not a feeling. When the word of God says to give honor to whom honor is due, it is not saying to wait until the atmosphere is conducive, just agree to it and let God handle the rest. Do your part. *Honour all men, Love the brotherhood, fear God, honour the king (1Peter 2:17).* This affirmation is not just in word but in deed. God commands us to respect each other and respect those who are in authority over us. At times it maybe difficult, but in any area where respect and trust is undeserved, it can be done through the Holy Spirit.

"I am your servant"—This speaks to Elijah's spirit and attitude, his posture.

Although Elijah was a great prophet and well known in that time, he never lifted himself above God, nor the people of God. He knew who God was and He knew his place. "I am your servant"…what powerful words. *Obey those who rule over you, and be submissive, for they watch out for your souls, as those who must give account. Let them do so with joy and not with grief, for that would be unprofitable for you (Hebrews 13:17 NKJV).*

Elijah was a servant to God and he was also a servant to the people of God. No matter what position or titles you hold, spouse, parent, community leader, manager, supervisor, pastor, ministry leader, deacon, elder, usher, etc., your posture should always be like Elijah "I AM YOUR SERVANT! *Submit to one another out of reverence to Christ (Eph. 5:21 NIV).* When we position ourselves under the authorities God has placed in our lives, God exalts us to high places. In the body of Christ we do not like to think of ourselves as under someone but that is the order of God. If God sees that we can bow to another that just exemplifies our ability to bow to Him. Humility is an asset not a liability, it does not take from you it is a character building experience that places you in positions of honor with the "Master." God will Honor and favor you if you possess the right posture; spirit and attitude.

"I have done all…at your word" = *obedience*

Elijah not only recognized who God was, and knew his place, but he was confident in his relationship with God, *"I have done all…at your word."* This was not a statement by a quitter, pretender or by someone who was uncommited. This was a statement by a man who obeyed the voice of God. Obedience as a whole should not be contingent on relationships, feelings, personality, age, gender, race or denomination. God calls us to obey. Nevertheless, obedience is a heart issue and does speak to our love for God. *And this is love, that we walk in obedience to his commands. As you have heard from the beginning; his command is that you love (2 John 6 NKJV).* We all are going to experience moments in our lives where the choice of exercising humility will be challenging. Humility will open an avenue that will allow the spirit of God to manifest himself in an unusual way. Humility is a very powerful tool that deems itself profitable to everyone who will operate within it.

Prayer

Hear me, O Lord, hear me, that this people may know that You are the Lord God, and that You have turned their hearts back to you again."

You cannot be a woman or man of worship without being a person of prayer. Prayer is your personal expression to God, and it gives God an avenue to communication with you. Without a prayer life you cannot be a worshipper.

While writing this book my mom passed away. It was and still is, a very difficult experience. While growing up I often heard my mother pray for her children. She seemed to have prayed for us more than she prayed for herself. My mom's favorite song was "I know prayer changes things." She not only sang it but believed it and everyone of her children are walking with the Lord.

Elijah prayed with total dependence on God. His plea was that God would hear and move so the people would know that He is God. What an unselfish prayer! This prayer was not for personal wants and needs, it was a prayer for the salvation and restoration of God's people. Our personal petitions can be great and seem insurmountable at times, so it is alright to seek God for yourself , but those prayers should not be the only ones we seek God for. James 5:16 says when we pray for each other we are healed. Are you experiencing answers to prayers? If not, could it be that you are to self absorbed and not considering the needs of others? God will heal, provide, and perform miracles when we pray for one another. Put the needs of others before yourself. When we pray for the needs of others God will see to it that our needs are met. It's a win, win situation.

Fire And Salvation

Then the fire of the Lord fell and consumed the burnt sacrifice, and wood and the stones and the dust, and it licked up the water that was in the trench.

Now when all the people saw it, they fell on their faces; and they said, "The Lord, He is God! The Lord, He is God!"

What a demonstration of power! God did not only move, but caused the people to call on Him. He will come through in the most impossible circumstances.

The thing that was interesting to me in this verse was the fire which represented the power of God, first acknowledged the sacrifice. The Holy Spirit spoke something to me in this verse that I want to share with you. Whatever you are waiting for God to do, or if there is an area in your life you need God to move in, ask yourself two questions. "Am I willing to make a sacrifice?" Great sacrifices brings great results. Secondly, ask yourself, "Will

God's name be made known in the end?" If the answer to those two questions is yes, you will experience a move of God.

God was so ready to pour out His spirit, you can almost feel the anticipation in this verse. Humor me in this analogy…God was in rare form that day. He saw Elijah's heart and He saw what Elijah did and He was excited! Conditions were met and at the end of Elijah's prayer of humility, He was ready! He burst through the clouds like a ball of fire and fell to the earth. He rose up and devoured the sacrifice, wood, stone and dirt, and with his tongue He licked up the water/word, which I believed He enjoyed the most. Then after that He filled the atmosphere with his presence and the people fell on their faces, worshipped and proclaimed Him as Lord and Savior. Although I paraphrased the verse a bit, the unusual presence of God is just that awesome and more!

God wants to perform in that way everyday if we let Him. He longs to devour our sacrifices and bless us. Can we sacrifice our time, skip some meals, turn off the television and our phones? Can we limit other entertainment devices and get alone with God by any means necessary? Purpose in our heart to make sacrifices as you live a life of worship to your King. God hungers for us like we hunger for him. When we stand corporately before Him in worship, He longs to see sacrifice. What sacrifices do we make in the congregation corporately as worshippers? The word of God in *Hebrews 13:15-16* calls them *"spiritual sacrifices,"* fruit of our lips, giving thanks to God, doing good and sharing. Open up your mouth and sing to the Lord, lift your hands and your hearts in thanks to Him, bring an offering to the Lord, share your testimony, these are examples of *"spiritual sacrifices"* we can do corporately.

Keep in mind, sacrifice is never about what we feel like doing but always about what God wants to do through us. God yearns to give us, a spiritual visitation by the Holy Spirit that will not only bless us but call Gods people to repentance.

If my people who are called by my name will humble themselves and pray and seek my face and turn from their wicked ways THEN I will hear from heaven, and forgive their sins and heal their land (2Chronicles 7:14 NKJV).

Chapter VII

Worship Etiquette
Tips for the Worship Leader

Worship Etiquette may sound strange to some of you. You may venture to say there is no such thing as worship etiquette, but I beg to differ. Etiquette is basically conduct, and I believe there is a certain conduct Worship Leaders and Praise and Worship teams must portray in order to be effective in leading a congregation into the presence of God. Worship is contagious. If you are excited about who you serve, it will cause other believers to be excited as well. For those who are not believers it will get their attention and to say the least, they will become curious. Remember that you are a demonstrator of worship. What you do, they (the congregation) will do.

Here are a few tips for training Praise and Worship teams, that Worship Leaders should be conscious of before standing in front of a congregation.

> 1. Stand confident. When you stand before the people confident and sure, it makes them feel comfortable about you and a level of trust builds. It is easy for someone to follow you if they believe you know what you are doing and is confident about who you are singing or talking about.

> 2. Be prepared. Rehearsal is key to effective worship leading. Have your music and songs prepared. Fumbling through songs and music will cause you to lose the confidence of your congregation.

3. Always wear a smile and look nice and neat. Give people something pleasant to look at. You are representing the almighty God, look pleasant and friendly and look your best. Looking your best helps people feel good about you and themselves.

4. Never come out of worship mode. Worship at all times. What I mean is, during the worship service raise your hands or mimic the leader. If you are between songs or during moments of silence, if the leader is praying, talking, or reading a scripture, stay worshipful, prayerful, clasp your hands together in front of you, close your eyes, or talk silently to God. Never just stand there watching the people, looking at each other or staring aimlessly into space.

5. Arms should never be folded in front of you. Keep them free unless you are holding a microphone.

6. No nervous rocking back and forth. Sway to the music only. When you appear nervous it makes your congregation nervous about you.

7. No picking your nails or adjusting any clothing. Take a quick "look over" before coming before the congregation.

These maybe "no brainers," but you would be surprised in my twenty plus years of doing worship how many people are guilty of these minor infractions. Appearance is important because appearance can be distracting especially if you want to keep your audience engaged.

Chapter VIII

Worship Service Format

Rejoice in the Lord, O you righteous! For praise from the upright is beautiful. Ps.33:1 NKJV

Setting the atmosphere for the Spirit of God to move is the job of the worship team and a very vital part of the worship service. If the atmosphere is not conducive it can hinder the Spirit of God. The following is just a general worship service format. You may use a different format based on the needs of your Pastor and congregation or maybe you do not have one at all. Nevertheless, before you prepare a format, talk to your pastor to see if there are any topics, special themes, or any special song requests. Then spend some time in the presence of the Lord for direction. The worship format that I am going to share is one I have used and have found to be very effective. Feel free to use it or use it as a guideline to create your own.

Call To Worship

At the beginning of any service there's a lot of commotion, people coming and going, talking, visiting and greeting one another. The call to worship segment is meant to bring order, to get everyone's attention and to invite them to stop what they are doing and come and worship the Lord. It is relative to a school bell ringing, letting the students know class is beginning. The song lyrics should not only be inviting, but it would be beneficial if the lyrics told the audience to do some sort of worship gesture. This will help them become engaged in worship. For example , Oh give thanks to the Lord; Clap your hands all ye people; Sing to the Lord a song of Praise: Lift your hands and bless

Him, Come and gather before our King or even "How great thou art" the key is to get their attention. The song choice here can be either a slow song or one of an upbeat rhythm.

Engagement

This stage can make or break your worship service. It is crucial that your audience is engaged at this point. When the audience is engaged, meaning they are participating in worship, standing, singing, clapping, or hands raised, God has the opportunity to work on the hearts of the people. Be very sensitive to the Spirit at this point. Although you have already prepared a schedule of songs to sing, God may have you stop and pray or read a scripture, again be sensitive to the spirit and join Him in what He is doing. If the audience is not engaged or if you sense something hindering the spirit from moving, it is either the enemy causing distraction, or the leader or a team member is not where they need to be spiritually. I mentioned in earlier chapters you cannot take the congregation where you have not been. It is very important that you silently surrender your spirit to God and ask God to reveal to you what is needed at this point. This is why it is very important that the leader and the worship team have a relationship with God so that he/she can hear from Him. Engagement gives the Spirit of God an opportunity to envelope your worship service and it welcomes the word to speak to the people.

Exaltation /Admiration

But thou art holy, O thou that inhabitest the praises of Israel. (Psalm 22:3).

I will praise the name of God with a song, and will magnify Him with thanksgiving.

This also shall please the Lord better than an ox or bull. (Ps. 69:30-31).

After the congregation is engaged in worship be intentional in calling and blessing the name of the Lord in song or in exhortation. Talk about how great He is and how thankful you are to Him for what He has done, and your expectancy of what He will do. God dwells and lives in the praises of His people. It pleases God when we call on His name. When we exalt and give honor to the Lord it makes Him feel good, it gets His attention, His face turns toward us, and He meets every need. As a parent, when your children speak well of you, it makes you feel loved, valued and appreciated. When you feel that your children appreciate you, sometimes you sacrifice for them or go that extra mile to do special things for them. I want to share letters I received from my sons. It was not for any particular occasion they just wanted to share some things with me.

>Dear Mom,
>
>Thank you so much for supporting me through everything I do. I would not be where I am if it were not for you (and God of course). I love you very much and I would not want to have anyone else for a mother. I hope that you are as proud to be my mother as I am to be your son!!!
>
>Love,
>
>Jason.

This next letter is from my youngest son, again not for any occasion.

> Dear Mom,
>
> Thank you for putting up with us even though we always do not see "feet to feet" (he has a sense of humor). Thank you for not giving up on us and for not leaving us after the divorce. Thanks for forgiving us when we did you wrong. Thanks for in stilling in us Godly and many qualities that will help us succeed in the future. Thank you for introducing us to salvation.
>
> Sincerely,
>
> Joshua Newman.

I cannot explain to you the joy that filled my heart when I received these words of admiration. What parent would not sacrifice and shower their children with blessings after hearing such gratefulness. God feels the exact same way when His children give glory to his name from a grateful heart. Exalt the Lord, shower Him with words of affirmation and adoration then watch God turn His face toward you and your congregation, and meet every need.

Intimacy

Call unto me, and I will answer thee and show thee great and mighty things, which thou knowest not. (Jeremiah 33:3 NKJV).

This is exactly what happens after you begin to call on the name of the Lord during worship. God will visit you. The intimacy portion of your worship time is what the Lord waits for. It is a very active, quiet time during worship when the spirit of the Lord walks through the congregation giving instructions, healing, restoring, saving, rescuing and revealing. He responds to every heart that has called upon Him. Suggested songs should be ones that ask the Holy Spirit to do something specific. It is important for the worship leader as well as the musicians to be still and sensitive to the direction of the Holy Spirit. A special song may be needed to encourage the moving of the spirit. My advice is that you never end your worship time before intimacy. Ground work is usually laid at this intimacy stage so that when the word of God is taught or preached there is nothing prohibiting it.

Chapter IX

Are You Ready To Be A Worship Leader

But let a man examine himself...(1Cor. 11:28)

Gifts and talents will bring you before the people but character will keep you there. In this letter to Corinth, Paul urges them to examine themselves. Take a honest look at your spiritual life, are you fit to lead? Notice, I did not ask are you perfect? Being fit here means is your heart right? Do you have the right motives? Do you feel called to the worship ministry and are you ready? *2 Tim. 2:15* says Study to show yourself approved unto God. Take the time and get before the Lord and let Him put His stamp of approval on your life. It matters not how well you can sing, it matters how well you can live. Remember you represent Christ. Are you giving Him a good name? Are you drawing people to Him or away from Him? As you ponder these questions I mentioned, take a look at the following list and see if there are any areas you need to surrender to the Lord. Examine yourself, what type of worship leader are you?

1. Sensitive to Authority.
2. Spends time with the Lord.
3. Have regular rehearsals.
4. Relational with worship team and is committed to their growth.
5. Pretends to have a worship life and goes through the motions.
6. Uses religious phrases and gestures to appear spiritual.
7. Takes worship seriously.
8. Prefers not to be seen.
9. Seeks to be seen and heard.
10. Demonstrates worship by worshipping.

11. Worships with a passion and heart for God
12. Draws attention to self by dressing too revealing or strange.
13. Talking too much with focus on personal experience
14. Leads by example.
15. Music and singing too loud.
16. Manipulates by working the crowd and pressuring them to respond.
17. Inflexible with the worship order; does everything according to plan.
18. Scopes the crowd for signs of approval.
19. Monopolizes the microphone.
20. Exalts the name of the Lord.
21. Entertaining by exaggerated movements when playing instrument or displaying vocal ability.
22. Gives honor and glory to God.

The message version of *John 4:23* interprets a worshipper like this; *But the time is coming it has in fact, come when what you're called will not matter and where you go to worship will not matter. It's who you are and the way you live that count before God. Your worship must engage your spirit in the pursuit of truth. That's the kind of people the father is out looking for: those who are simply and honestly themselves before him in their worship. God is sheer being itself Spirit. Those who worship Him must do it out of their very being, their spirits, their true selves, in adoration.*

Worship is such an extraordinary gift given to mankind. There is nothing created that comes close to worship. It is powerful, sacred and liberating. Worship cannot be imitated, worship must be practiced. When worship is exercised, your enemies will flee, chains will fall and mountains will become level plains. The blind will see and those who are lame will walk again. A life that worships will have peace with God, with themselves and with others. My prayer, is after reading this book, you allow God to stir up the gift of worship that is within you.

A Woman/Man Of Worship

Joshua Newman

A woman/man of worship is a glorious attribute
The only thing that keeps them from being depressed
heartbroken and destitute
But how do you start, where do you begin?
Is worship something that burst from within?
Is it something that comes forth when we need it the most
or is it a spiritual talent from God of which no man should
boast?
No! worship is praise that gives life meaning and purpose
That makes us realize that we are inadequate and imperfect
Only then can we immerse our being in the awe of His
glory
That humbles and teaches us that we will never be worthy
When this revelation becomes clear and we can begin to
piece together God's clue
That the hour is coming when true worshippers must
worship him in spirit and in truth.

Made in the USA
Charleston, SC
17 August 2014